A PATH,
A PRAYER
and
GOD'S PRESENCE

A PATH,
A PRAYER
and
GOD'S PRESENCE

AN ANTHOLOGY OF POETRY AND
INSPIRATIONAL MESSAGES

PHYLLIS L WERNSING

A PATH, A PRAYER AND GOD'S PRESENCE
AN ANTHOLOGY OF POETRY AND
INSPIRATIONAL MESSAGES

iUniverse books may be ordered through booksellers or by contacting:

iUniverse
1663 Liberty Drive
Bloomington, IN 47403
www.iuniverse.com
1-800-Authors (1-800-288-4677)

Because of the dynamic nature of the Internet, any web addresses or links contained in this book may have changed since publication and may no longer be valid. The views expressed in this work are solely those of the author and do not necessarily reflect the views of the publisher, and the publisher hereby disclaims any responsibility for them.

Any people depicted in stock imagery provided by Thinkstock are models, and such images are being used for illustrative purposes only.
Certain stock imagery © Thinkstock.

ISBN: 978-1-4759-0103-0 (sc)
ISBN: 978-1-4759-0104-7 (e)

Printed in the United States of America

iUniverse rev. date: 12/09/2014

This book is dedicated to the glory of God and

to those who prayerfully take time to see, hear, feel and

know the presence of God.

Photographs by Phyllis

CONTENTS

A PATH, A PRAYER AND GOD'S PRESENCE

There are times when we are told by family, friends, clergy, and others that God is always with us.

Let us embrace that thought for a moment.

Many of us have a place where nature can be found. We may be able to walk beside a lake, walk through a park, garden, greenway or simply enjoy our own backyards where flowers, birds, squirrels, trees and nature is abundant.

Being close to nature brings me close to God, but do not think God is found only in nature for God sits beside you where you are and where you are is where you will find God.

One day I went to a Bog Garden where nature is very plentiful during all seasons of the year. As I sat to enjoy what was before me, I felt the breath of God within the wind. The path before me was clear and I felt God speak within my heart. He seemed to want me to invite you to listen as we walked and prayed together.

Listen for God within your heart, mind and being.

Join me as I pray.

Feel God's presence as He whispers your name.

Hear what He has to say within the pages of A PATH, A PRAYER AND GOD'S PRESENCE.

Proverbs 2:1-10 RSV

MY SON, if you receive my words and treasure up my commandments with you, making your ear attentive to wisdom and inclining your heart to understanding; yes, if you cry out for insight and raise your voice for understanding, if you seek it like silver and search for it as for hidden treasures, then you will understand the fear of the LORD and find the knowledge of God. For the LORD gives wisdom; from his mouth come knowledge and understanding; he stores up sound wisdom for the upright, he is a shield to those who walk in integrity, guarding the paths of justice and preserving the way of his saints. Then you will understand righteousness and justice and equity, every good path; for wisdom will come into your heart, and knowledge will be pleasant to your soul.

I AM HUMAN

I am human and often don't hear.
Please forgive me when You shout in deaf ears.

I am human and often can't see.
Please forgive me when I'm wrapped up in me.

I am human and often don't feel.
Please forgive me and teach me to heal.

I am human and often don't share.
Please forgive me because I really do care.

I am human and often I'm weak.
Please forgive me and give me Your strength.

This is my prayer Lord.
I pray it to You.

Use it Your way Lord.
However You choose. Amen.

1 Kings 8:30 RSV
And hearken thou to the supplication of thy servant and of thy people Israel, when they pray toward this place; yea, hear thou in heaven thy dwelling place; and when thou hearest, forgive.

HE LOOKED INTO
MY EYES

I saw a tattered house.

As I watched, someone walked up the un-kept path and knocked on the door. A person opened the door and the joy that came over her was unmistakable. The person approaching the door stayed for a few minutes and then walked back down the path. It was then I saw the flowers in the arms of the person who opened the door.

A friend walked out of the tattered house and came to me. He looked into my eyes and said: "The person on the path should be you. A heart filled with flowers is a heart filled with love. So it is with everyone."

Thank you Lord for reminding me to give love to those in need. Amen.

Deuteronomy 13:4 NIV
It is the LORD your God you must follow, and him you must revere. Keep his commands and obey him; serve him and hold fast to him.

GOD'S LIFE

The New Year is on the horizon of my calendar and I find myself thinking of days gone by as well as the days before me. I am tempted to wander through the days gone by with you, but I will not. I am also tempted to speculate on the year ahead, but I will not. I will simply pray for our thoughts as we enter into another year.

Before I begin my thoughts, let me ask: Exactly when does a new year begin? Does a new year begin at the start of a new calendar or does it start each day we put our feet before us . . . one step at a time?

As I was praying, I felt a tug at my heart strings. Silently, I listened and I heard this beautiful thought within my heart and my mind:

"Does God participate in your lives or do you participate in God's life?"

An interesting thought . . . don't you think? So often our thoughts seem to be misled. We seem to feel as if God was created for us.

This is not so.

We were created for God. We were created out of God's great love for us. Let us remember that God loved us so much that He saved us through his Son Jesus.

Genesis 1:27 NKJV

So God created man in His own image; in the image of God He created him; male and female He created them.

SIMPLE THINGS

I am a nature photographer and I travel from place to place taking photos of many types of nature. Have you ever taken a few minutes to look deeply into the creation of a flower? Their beauty goes much deeper than the surface of their creation.

Birds are created in their own creative way.

Animals come to us in the greatness of the One that created them.

Look upon nature and see yourself within its creation.

Simple things are not created lightly for their creation is as complex as the complexity of its Creator. Picture what the Creator has placed before you and remember its beauty.

Lamentations 3:25 NLT
The Lord is good to those who wait for Him, to the one who looks for Him.

I THINK GOD SMILES!

I have a cat named Pebbles that is quite independent. Pebbles does her own thing and she goes her own way. She mostly does what she wants to do when she wants to do it and she rarely needs someone to give her praise or attention. Although Pebbles needs little from others, there **are** days that she will hunt me down and curl up on my lap.

Today is one of those days.

Pebbles is curled into a little ball . . . purring as she settles into contentment.

What joy I feel as this independent cat trusts me this morning! What love I have for her even when she watches me from a distance . . . My love does not change even when she is distant and cold!

I wonder if that is how God feels about us. Do you think God smiles when we trust Him enough to come into His presence for rest? I do!

I think God smiles each time we seek Him out for rest and comfort . . . just as Pebbles seeks me out for comfort from time to time.

Just as I love Pebbles when she is being independent and watches me from afar, God also loves us when we are being independent and watch Him from afar. His love for us never changes.

Genesis 1:26-27 NRSV

Then God said, "Let us make humankind in our image, according to our likeness; and let them have dominion over the fish of the sea, and over the birds of the air, and over the cattle, and over all the wild animals of the earth, and over every creeping thing that creeps upon the earth." So God created humankind in his image, in the image of God he created them; male and female he created them.

A Time to Pray

My heart belongs to You, Lord Jesus. Please hold it gently within Your hands. In Your Name I pray. Amen.

Dear Jesus, You are the road to God. If I follow You, will You lead me to Him . . . or will You lead me elsewhere until I am able to follow You with all my heart and soul? Amen.

REMEMBER...

Psalm 23: 4 NLT

> *Even when I walk through the dark valley of death, I will not be afraid, for you are close beside me. Your rod and your staff protect and comfort me.*

I decided to take a late night walk. The stars were bright and beautiful. I walked in silence because my silence seemed to be comforting me this night. As I walked, I began to feel as if the Lord was walking with me in the darkness. It seemed that I could feel His presence and hear His words. What I heard in my heart was:

"I go before you. I am behind you. I walk beside you. Take my hand and walk with Me. There is nothing to fear because we walk together. We walk in the light even in the midst of darkness. Remember . . . death can snatch away life like the darkness descending upon the darkest of night, but I stand watch and protect my own.

Beware for there are many ways to die . . . even in life. Amen.

THE KNOWLEDGE
YOU HAVE

I saw people putting something together.

They seemed to be quite quick in their movements, but at the end of the project . . . not much fit together. I wondered about what I saw before me. Before I asked my question, a friend offered this expiation:

"To do anything well, it takes time, patience, courage and knowledge."

"How well you are able to do something depends on how much knowledge you have at that point in life. If time, patience and courage are needed, then with knowledge, they too are added."

Psalm 4:6 NRSV
There are many who say, "O that we may see some good! Let the light of your face shine on us, O LORD."

THE LION

I sat in prayer. My thoughts were with a friend that had been going through some rough times. As I prayed for her and her situation, I saw an image within my thoughts. I became aware of words spoken within my thoughts and I wrote those words in my journal. I feel this message is for my friend, but it is important for all of us to understand the message as well.

This is what I wrote: I see the image of "The Lion" in the darkness of myself. His eyes are deep and penetrating. The bridge of his nose is wide and his strength is felt within my being. His soft fur beckons me to nestle deep within its soft touch. The darkness fades into itself and I rest in the care of "My Lord." Amen.

Close your eyes my friend.

The Lion of Judah waits for you as well as for me.

Rest my friend. Rest.

Amen.

Revelation 5:4-5 NIV

I wept and wept because no one was found who was worthy to open the scroll or look inside. Then one of the elders said to me, "Do not weep! See, the Lion of the tribe of Judah, the Root of David, has triumphed. He is able to open the scroll and its seven seals."

THE RIGHT KEY

I stood before a beautiful door. A large key was in my hand. I could see that this key would not fit into the lock on the door. Puzzled, I wondered where I could find the correct key. As I turned to search for another key, I saw my friend resting under a tree. As I sat beside him, I asked why the key in my hand did not work. I told him that this key had opened other doors and I was certain that it would work on this door as well. He smiled and gently said:

"You have to use the right key in order to open the right door. The key to the house will not open the door to the car. So it is with spiritual things."

Lord, forgive me when I try to use the wrong keys at the wrong time. I know that you have provided us with many keys to open the doors before us. Help me to use prayer when that key is needed. Help me to read the Bible daily and let me speak your Word with boldness. I know these keys are only a few of Your keys, but to me they are keys that will help me open the right door at the right time. In You will I trust. Amen.

Psalm 33:4 RSV
For the word of the LORD is upright; and all his work is done in faithfulness.

GRAIN

There is beauty within the grain.
It is touched by wind and rain.
The grain will bend to cloudy skies.
And then it stands very high.
Yes, the wind and rain can only bend it.
And man will always come to claim it.

Proverbs 3:9-10 NIV
  Honor the LORD with your wealth, with the firstfruits of all your crops; then your barns will be filled to overflowing, and your vats will brim over with new wine.

DO YOU CARE?

Do you care for the world around you as much as God cares for you and your world? Think for a moment . . . do you take care of what has been given to you? You may say yes, but look again into the folds of your life. Were you given talents of art, music, translating languages, friendship, praying, knowledge, reading books to others?

The list goes on and on.

Do you use those talents?

Do you take care of your home, money, the garden, yourself?

The list goes on and on. Do you take care of those blessings?

We are all called to take care of what has been given to us by the One that created us.

So, rest if you need to rest.

Run when you need to run, but keep your focus on the care you give to all things that God has given to you in its proper proportion.

Remember . . . Care for what God has given to you and you will see how much God cares for you.

Tell me, how much do **you** care?

2 Timothy 4:7-8 KJV

I have fought a good fight, I have finished my course, I have kept the faith; Henceforth there is laid up for me a crown of righteousness, which the Lord, the righteous judge, shall give me at that day: and not to me only, but unto all them also that love his appearing.

Lord, please be with me as I go through this day.
Just kind of puttering as I go my way.
I know You will show me where to go and what to say.
I pray you will stop me if I start to stray.
Thank You Lord for your unending Love. Amen.

LET US PRAY

I know the Lord is with me today.
I hear the words He wants me to say.

I hear His voice in all that I do.
His voice is with me as well as with you.

Let us together hear what He might say.
Together we'll know as we kneel here to pray.

We'll lift up our voices in silence and say:
Fill me with You, Lord. Show me Your way.

He'll send us His love. He'll lead us today.
If we'll kneel together and continue to pray.

Psalm 40:6 RSV
> *Sacrifice and offering thou dost not desire; but thou hast given me an open ear. Burnt offering and sin offering thou hast not required.*

SEASONS

I sat thinking about life.

Why are there seasons for us all, I wondered?

An answer to my question entered my thoughts:

"If there were no seasons for us, we would not experience the variety of life we now have. If we all ate at the same time, there soon would be famine. If we all served at the same time, there soon would be no one to be served."

"There are seasons for us all . . . a time to serve, a time to harvest and a time to grow. Where are you in your time of seasons?"

Thank you Lord for the seasons of life as well as the seasons of the world. Amen.

Psalm 67:6 NIV
  Then the land will yield its harvest, and God,
our God, will bless us.

INFINITE RESPECT

I was in a meeting and I did not feel comfortable with everyone attending the meeting.

Concerned about my feelings, I took a minute to pray. Within my heart I thought I heard some words that expressed wisdom. Let me share those thoughts with you. This is what I heard: "You do not need to be like everyone, but everyone should be given respect. Infinite respect is a gift unto all. Infinite respect is of God and men simply hold onto respect as a torch given unto them in the darkness of time."

My thoughts returned to the meeting with renewed interest.

I realize that I may not agree with everyone, but I can listen to what is said with the same respect I would want others to give to me.

Thank you Lord for showing me that everyone deserves respect and as I know this in my heart . . . I do not always practice it in my thoughts. Forgive me Lord. Amen.

1 Peter 3:13-15 RSV

Now who is there to harm you if you are zealous for what is right? But even if you do suffer for righteousness' sake, you will be blessed. Have no fear of them, nor be troubled, but in your hearts reverence Christ as Lord. Always be prepared to make a defense to anyone who calls you to account for the hope that is in you, yet do it with gentleness and reverence.

A BOUNTIFUL CROP

I felt as if I were looking out a window of an airplane. As I looked at the fields below, I felt the presence of someone beside me. Turning to the person beside me, I recognized a friend. He smiled and said:

"I see the patchwork of fields before me and I wonder if they will receive what they need to produce a bountiful crop. Sun, rain, nutrients and faith are needed for the fields to bear the gifts within them. If this is true for the fields, how much more do I expect of you?"

I will trust in you Lord Jesus for all that I need. Amen.

Jeremiah 31:12 NAS
"And they shall come and shout for joy on the height of Zion, And they shall be radiant over the bounty of the LORD—Over the grain, and the new wine, and the oil. And over the young of the flock and the herd; And their life shall be like a watered garden, And they shall never languish again.

QUESTIONS

Genesis 17:7 NIV
I will establish my covenant as an everlasting covenant between me and you and your descendants after you for the generations to come, to be your God and the God of your descendants after you.

As I read my Bible, my thoughts began to wander. I stopped my reading to hear what was being said within those thoughts. I sat in quiet reflection for a few moments and was able to hear what I was to hear. Let me share what I heard: "The questions of the world are answered by the generations to come. How will they answer those questions set before them?"

That is a good question.

How will the generations to come answer questions about Jesus and what He did for all of us? I have heard that many of our children are not involved in church or any other bible-related program.

We are in jeopardy of losing generations of children to the way of the world. We are in jeopardy of allowing answers to fade into the folds of time.

How will we retrieve the children of the world from a world that can cause so much sorrow and pain?

I suppose the answer is that **we** will not retrieve the children of the world from a world such as it is today or even tomorrow. Jesus will be the one to place love within the hearts of the children of generations to come. Jesus is the one that has always placed the need for one generation to show the next generation how to answer the questions set before them, but we are not off the hook any more than the generations of the Bible. We must continue to be examples of Jesus Christ our Lord. The generations set before us is within the hand of God.

Lord Jesus, help us to reflect You to those within our reach and help us pray for the generations past as well as the generation of years to come. Amen.

MY COMFORT ZONE

As I thought about stepping out of my comfort zone, my thoughts wandered. I began to think about comfort zones.

Exactly what task do I consider "out of my comfort zone?"

To be honest, I am still working on the answer to the question set before me and hopefully I will think about that question long after I have identified my current comfort zone.

As I thought about life and all it holds for me to participate in, I realized that in any moment, I could be asked to do or participate in something I really am uncomfortable in doing.

But wait . . . Isn't stepping out of my comfort zone doing exactly that . . . doing something different from what I usually do?

I continued with my thinking.

As I thought, I felt a tug within my heart.

I stopped to listen to what was within my heart. This is what I heard: "You can move mountains in your mind. You can create peace in your thoughts. You can love the unlovable with your heart and as you do all these things, you can do nothing without God."

How true that thought is!

I think I will put God first in my thoughts and prayers concerning "my comfort zone" . . . knowing He will lead me to the right place for me to serve.

What about you?

Do you ever think about stepping out of your comfort zone and doing something really wild or helpful? What exactly would you do? Where is God leading you to serve?

Thank you Lord for showing me where you need my help. Amen.

> Philippians 1:6 KJV
>   Being confident of this very thing, that he which hath begun a good work in you will perform it until the day of Jesus Christ.

MY LIFE IS RESTORED

Psalm 123:1-4 NRSV
> *To you I lift up my eyes,*
> > *O you who are enthroned in the heavens!*
> *As the eyes of servants*
> > *look to the hand of their master,*
> *as the eyes of a maid*
> > *to the hand of her mistress,*
> *so our eyes look to the LORD our God,*
> > *until he has mercy upon us.*
> *Have mercy upon us, O LORD, have mercy upon us,*
> > *for we have had more than enough of contempt.*
> *Our soul has had more than its fill*
> > *of the scorn of those who are at ease,*
> > *of the contempt of the proud.*

Have mercy on me LORD that I will see You within this Psalm. Amen.

Forgive me LORD if I have been one of those who have been seen as proud. I grieve over their contempt for me and I pray that Your forgiveness will restore me unto their favor.

I lift my eyes unto You . . . You who are enthroned in the heavens.

I see Your glory before me and my life is restored. Amen.

A GOOD THOUGHT

I read these words within one of the notebooks that I had written over the past twenty seven years: We run from God . . . until we find Him. I am not quite sure what I was thinking at the time I wrote those thoughts, but they still seem to hold true today.

I remember the day I began to trust God.

You may be able to remember the day you began to trust God and then again, you might feel as if God has always been with you. Either way, I am sure we can all relate to a time in our lives that we seemed to run from God.

No matter how fast we run or how far we run . . . we will always find God waiting for us. We cannot outrun God. We cannot hide from God. We cannot leave God because God will not leave us!

I wonder if I had the same thought the day I wrote it into my notebook. I must say that the thought I had then is still as good as thoughts I have today.

Thank you Lord. Amen.

Joshua 1:9 NRSV
"Be strong and courageous; do not be frightened or dismayed, for the LORD your God is with you wherever you go."

OUR GIFTS

Many times we refer to the things of the Spirit as gifts.

I have been in classes that helped us identify "our gifts." What exactly do people mean when they refer to "gifts?"

Some teachers of my classes would say something like "You have a gift for teaching." You may even be told that your gifts lie in working with older adults. Your gifts may be in the arts like music or painting. The list could get very long and so, I will refrain from telling you about the gifts that are available to you because "the gifts" God has given to us are endless.

In reality . . . Life in itself is a gift.

What we enjoy doing **are** our gifts.

Accept your gift for what it is because it is what it is to enjoy.

Lord, sometimes we find that some things we are asked to do in life we may not enjoy. Help us see You in all of life . . . that in itself is a gift from You. Amen.

> *1 Corinthians 14:12 NIV*
> *So it is with you. Since you are eager to have spiritual gifts, try to excel in gifts that build up the church.*

HIS DAY

This is the day the Lord has made. I will rejoice and be glad in it . . .
For the Lord has allowed me to join Him in His day.

Forgive me Lord because I do not always remember to rejoice in Your day. Amen.

This day is a gift of grace that God created for all of us, but I do not always remember that He created it . . . not me. Sometimes I get all wrapped up in my own thinking. Once I am caught up in my own thinking, I find myself trying to tie the bow on what I thought I created. (Which is not an easy feat.)
Being all wrapped up in my own thinking takes me away from doing what the Lord really wants me to do with His day. Forgive me once again Lord. Amen.

I know I will be praying for forgiveness in the days before me Lord. Please help me to remember that You created each day. Amen.

Within my heart I could feel the Lord smile as He said "I am with you always."

Ephesians 4:7 KJV
But unto every one of us is given grace according to the measure of the gift of Christ.

THE BLOSSOM

As I prepared to create a photo book called "The Irises of High Point" I felt a tug at my thoughts. I clearly heard the thought placed within my thinking and I included the thought into my photo book . . . for thoughts can complement what we see in life.

This is what I put into my photo book:

The beauty of a flower must be experienced at the time of its glory . . . For its glory is seen briefly and the blossom returns unto its creator until creation returns in the Spring of each season.

Thank you Lord Jesus for the beautiful thoughts I found as I prepared a photo book of Irises. Amen.

2 Corinthians 2:15-16 NRSV
> *For we are the aroma of Christ to God among those who are being saved and among those who are perishing; to the one a fragrance from death to death, to the other a fragrance from life to life.*

GOD LOVED ME TODAY

God loved me today.
I saw Him in your smile.
He loved me once more
When you came to stay awhile.

God loved me today.
With a big bear hug.
He loved me once more
When my son shared his bug.

God loved me today.
I saw Him in the sky
He loved me once more
When a child asked why.

God loved me today.
I saw an old friend.
He loved me once more
As I made a new friend.

God loved me today.
He died for my sin.
God loved me once more
When He rose again.

Yes, God loved me today.
I know this is true.
He loved me once more
Because He also loved you.

BE MYSELF

I am to be where I am, who I am and allow God to direct my life. To be someone other than myself is to go against what God wants for me and that often accomplishes only what **I** want for myself.

> *Job 33:4 RSV*
> *The spirit of God has made me, and the breath of the Almighty gives me life.*

Lord, I give you my life this day. I'll let you use it in Your way. Forgive me when I think I am in control in any way. Amen.

OPEN YOUR EYES

I was with a friend.

We gazed upon many things.

We saw beauty, sorrow, death, and new life. We saw things of unspeakable beauty and we saw things that cut deeply into my heart. I longed to help in both areas.

My friend turned to me and said:

"What do you say about Him since He has opened your eyes?"

I was speechless. I was in awe of all that I had seen. After thinking for a moment, I was able to utter a few words. I looked at my friend and said: "He is Lord."

Jesus is truly Lord of all things and I feel that my friend and I will walk many miles together. Amen.

> *John 9:17 KJV*
> *They say unto the blind man again, What sayest thou of him, that he hath opened thine eyes? He said, He is a prophet.*

YOU

Sometimes I can get stuck on me to the extent that I forget you.

When I heard the words above within my thoughts, I quickly defended myself, but the words seemed to have truth within them. I do not know about you, but I get caught up in my own life . . . my health, my spiritual needs, my financial wellbeing, my family, etc., etc. I often focus on me and become unaware of you.

Forgive me Lord. How can I help You as well as all the you's You bring into my life? Amen.

Colossians 4:6 NAS
Let your speech always be with grace, seasoned, as it were, with salt, so that you may know how you should respond to each person.

FINDING LOVE

As I sat praying, my eyes were heavy with tears and the One that comforts me spoke these words within my heart:

"Among the rubble and clutter, beauty will spring forth. Out of your sorrow and grief a light will shine. There is good in everything. Look to see where the good is to be found. Is a flower growing nearby? Is a sunbeam peeking through the window? Is there a love that runs deep enough to suffer? We suffer for those we love. If you did not love them, then you could not suffer. Are you willing to continue to suffer for those you love? The old . . . and the new?"

"You are experiencing a new depth in Me."

"I know that you love many. They love you also. Let those who need your love receive it and they will receive it with an open heart. Do not be afraid to love for fear of suffering. Suffer with them and you will find love."

Luke 9:22 NIV
And he said, "The Son of Man must suffer many things and be rejected by the elders, chief priests and teachers of the law, and he must be killed and on the third day be raised to life."

FEEL HIS PRESENCE

Acts 2:22 KJV

Ye men of Israel hear these words; Jesus of Nazareth, a man approved of God among you by miracles and wonders and signs, which God did by him in the midst of you, as ye yourselves also know.

Actually studying scripture includes listening and feeling what that scripture might say to you. As I prepared for my Bible Study class, I felt the scripture above pulling me into its thoughts. This is what I received as I became woven into its beauty:

My Lord Jesus was approved by God and sent unto the earth to save the people of God that they do not die of sin. Many people die of many things, but Jesus died that we might not die of sin because He took the sin and died for us.

Until his death Jesus walked among the people of God for God created the people.

Jesus did many wonders and miracles while He walked through the streets of this world. Now walk the streets placed before **you** and feel His presence. Look for Him and know the power of where He walks today.

A GREAT FLOOD

Troubles rushed in like a great flood. They started like a small stream and grew to overwhelming proportions. Then the flood was gone and in the dry creek-bed stood My Lord. There was debris from the flood all around Him. He smiled and quietly started to clean up the destruction.

He said not one word, but peace and order came with My Lord. He knew. He chose to come into this day because He was needed. He chose to quiet the raging waters, not because I asked, but because of His love for me.

Let My Lord Jesus Christ enter the troubles of your day. The raging waters will quiet and peace will flow like a gentle stream.

Genesis 8:13 NKJV
And it came to pass in the six hundred and first year, in the first month, the first day of the month, that the waters were dried up from the earth; and Noah removed the covering of the ark and looked, and indeed the surface of the ground was dry.

CREATION

Spring has finally arrived on the calendar!

The winter was filled with many storms that brought snow and more snow to different parts of our country. All in all we had just enough snow in our area to make most of us happy and for that I am thankful.

I know that Winter has its own beauty, but I think Spring flowers and warmer weather is one of the highlights of creation. God certainly knew what He was doing when He created Spring and the beauty that will follow those dreary winter months. What a miracle to behold!

When creation is sprouting from within the darkness of winter, I begin to think of what a miracle it was when God created me from the darkness of the universe in which I lived. What a miracle it is to think that the God, who created the universe, loves me! I am but a speck of sand compared to all that surrounds me . . . and yet, God still loves me . . . just as I am! Oh, what miracles there are within the world surrounding the universe within.

Have you ever thought what a miracle it was when God created **you**? For surely, you are a miracle!

Genesis 22:17 NRSV
I will indeed bless you, and I will make your offspring as numerous as the stars of heaven and as the sand that is on the seashore.

ERASERS

Have you ever thought about an eraser? It is such a small part of our lives and yet, it is something useful and very unique.

Let's take a moment to think about erasers.

An eraser is such a small item, but it can correct large and small mistakes. When a person writes . . . mistakes can be made. Often those mistakes are not noticed until later and then they seem to pop out like a large boulder in a narrow path. Once we become aware of a mistake, we have the opportunity to pick up an eraser, make a correction and create order where there was confusion.

Jesus is like an eraser. We write out the story of our lives on a day to day basis and often mistakes are made. Some mistakes are noticed and some go unnoticed only to pop up later and create confusion. These mistakes can be corrected, but only when we pick up Jesus in our life and allow Him to create order where there was confusion.

Thank you Lord Jesus for erasers. I pray they do not be forgotten in a world of computers and cell phones. Amen.

Acts 19:32 RSV
Now some cried one thing, some another; for the assembly was in confusion, and most of them did not know why they had come together.

TEARS

God shed some tears so long ago.
Those tears were shed that we might know.
His love for us ran deep with pain.
His love for us will still remain.

His love for us was strong and true.
He gave his Son for me and you.

God shed some tears so long ago.
Those tears were shed that we might know.
His love for us ran very deep.
His love for us is ours to keep.

Those tears were shed in ages past.
Those tears were shed so they might last.

1 John 3:1 RSV
    See what love the Father has given us, that we
should be called children of God; and so we are.

EXPECTATIONS

I sat quietly. My thoughts wandered into areas of expectations. What exactly did I expect of myself? What do others expect of me? What will be expected of me if I had a publisher print my books? In addition to expectations about myself, what would I expect of others?

As I went through my thoughts, I felt as if someone challenged my thinking. Within my thoughts I heard "Expectations of ones-self should not spill over into the expectations of others. For expectations of ones-self is not usually a true reflection of reality."

Thank you Lord for inspiration, compassion and forgiveness. Amen.

Lamentations 3:22 NAS
The LORD's loving kindnesses indeed never cease, For His compassions never fail.

THE VOICE OF HEAVEN

I saw images of destruction.

Water ran wild across land that once grew crops. Wind blew homes from their foundations. I saw drought suck the life from all those searching for relief. I saw much more. I saw fire consume all in its path and woodland creatures ran for their lives.

I saw images of destruction.

I saw what we do to each other.

From the destruction a friend came to me. I heard him say, "When the great power of nature lifts His hand, we surely tremble beneath it. The Voice of Heaven can create the world . . . just as the world was created in the beginning."

As my Friend lifted his hand, I saw healing.

I saw water within its banks and people used the water to give each other drinks from cups of joy. The wind was calm as children across the land played in grass so green that woodland creatures danced with them and happiness was seen within each small face. The children became clear in my seeing. The children were you and I. We can choose the way of joy as we extend our lives unto the Voice of Heaven.

Sometimes we forget who is running the show and then something will happen to remind us. Create in us a clean heart O Lord. Amen.

Hebrews 10:21-22 NIV

.... and since we have a great priest over the house of God, let us draw near to God with a sincere heart in full assurance of faith, having our hearts sprinkled to cleanse us from a guilty conscience and having our bodies washed with pure water.

Lord, I wish I could be like You.
Lord, I wish I could see like You.
But I am human and I am unable to achieve such greatness. Forgive me for falling so short of what You would have me become and help me to strive to make each day a day of joy and beauty. Thank you Lord for this day. Amen.

Lord, I am not a perfect expression of perfection, but use me just as I am and in whatever way You can. Amen.

VISUALIZATION

I was in a Bible study where the person doing the devotional wanted us to try visualization. I thought "Here we go again! I will give it another try!"

You see, over the years several other people in Bible studies have attempted to get me to visualize quiet gardens, mountain tops and rivers. I have found that when I am asked to do this visualization . . . I am not able to do it. I am not sure why I cannot visualize what is asked of me, but I am not able to do what they would like me to do. Then again, when I am alone during my devotional time I am able to see what the Lord wants me to see.

One thing about visualization is that one must know where one is going. If you have not been in a beautiful garden, how can you picture the garden in your mind? Maybe you can picture someone else's experiences . . . Like looking at a painting or a photograph.

Do you know where you are going?

In order to experience visualization . . . it would be best to do some research for yourself. Maybe you could go to a garden. Does your city have a Botanical garden where you could sit and absorb the beauty around you? Can you smell the flowers? Do you hear the birds?

Absorb the presence of God. One need not go far to experience God. If you place a bird feeder in your backyard, the birds will come into your garden and sing songs of joy and thanksgiving. Experience God surrounding you and visualize His love.

Now that we have taken care of seeing a garden, why don't we try a mountain? Remember to go where God wants you to go . . . not where others may lead you.

Isaiah 58:11 RSV
And the LORD will guide you continually, and satisfy your desire with good things, and make your bones strong; and you shall be like a watered garden, like a spring of water, whose waters fail not.

UNTO HIMSELF

I saw a foot touch the earth's surface and as I watched . . . a hand touched people from all parts of the earth. As I pondered the meaning of what I saw, a friend placed his hand upon my shoulder and said:

"As the Lamb of God's foot touches the earth, so shall the ones He calls unto Himself shall be called and touched by His hand and no one shall keep them unto themselves for they shall see the face of all. And all shall not overtake that which is His."

> *Psalm 10:12 KJV*
> *Arise, O LORD; O God, lift up thine hand:*
> *forget not the humble.*

ALTARS

Joshua 22:26-28 RSV

Therefore we said, 'Let us now build an altar, not for burnt offering, nor for sacrifice, but to be a witness between us and you, and between the generations after us, that we do perform the service of the LORD in his presence with our burnt offerings and sacrifices and peace offerings; lest your children say to our children in time to come," You have no portion in the LORD." And we thought, If this should be said to us or to our descendants in time to come, we should say, 'Behold the copy of the altar of the LORD, which our fathers made, not for burnt offerings, nor for sacrifice, but to be a witness between us and you.'

What kind of altar are you building?

Do you build an altar for generations to come?

We may not build physical altars for generations that come after us, but surely we build spiritual altars for others to see. Is your altar being used in the right way? Do you sacrifice others on your altar or do you use your altar to pray for them? We each have choices concerning the altars we build. Let us look upon the altars built throughout our lives to see if they were built to serve as a witness to God.

WHAT DO YOU SEE?

As I traveled a rural road, I became aware of the rolling hills along the way. They seemed to come to life for me and I found myself passing the time by seeing different things in the sky and in the shadows on the hills. As I looked I heard these words within my heart:

"What do you see in life around you? One person is able to see an eagle with wings which cover an entire valley. Another can see a man's face carved by wind and rain. Still another may see a lady sunning herself while she gently blows the clouds above her head. Look around you and you may be able to see the image of God before you. If you do not look, you will not see. Open your eyes and heart to the things which are around you."

Genesis 1:31 KJV
And God saw everything that he had made, and, behold, it was very good. And the evening and the morning were the sixth day.

COLORS OF LIFE

I saw the leaves of summer.

As I watched the leaves blow within a gentle breeze, a friend spoke softly to me. I heard him tell me this truth from nature: "Some people say that the color green is the color of life, but I say it is not the only color of life. All that lives bears the colors of life."

"Look around you."

"Do you only see the color green or can you see the many colors before you?"

"Do you close your eyes to the life presented to you? Open your eyes . . . for there are many colors to life and life reflects many colors."

Romans 11:36 NRSV
For from him and through him and to him are all things. To him be the glory forever. Amen.

NEVER, NEVER LAND

Exodus 20:11 NAS
For six days the LORD made the heavens and
the earth, the seas and all that is in them, and rested
on the seventh day; therefore the LORD blessed the
sabbath day and made it holy.

One morning I was a volunteer answering the telephone at my church. I was trying to transfer a caller to our Pastors "voice mail box" when I pushed a wrong button and the person on the other end of the telephone went into never, never land! Oops! The caller was kind enough to call back. (Thank goodness!) When I explained what had happened, he laughed and said, "That's all right. It didn't hurt." I quickly pushed the right button and the caller was able to leave a message.

Do you think heaven has an answering machine with lots of buttons someone has to push as prayers come in? Do you think someone directs prayers to the correct areas?

Prayers for hospitals . . . Extension 102.

Prayers for sunny days . . . Extension 604.

Prayers for friends . . . Extension 007.

Well, you get the idea!

I wonder if heaven has a never, never land!

Remember as you pray that the Lord rested on the seventh day which is the Sabbath and holy. Knowing that the Sabbath is a day of rest makes me wonder . . . Do you think our prayers might be restful to the Lord.

Could our prayers be like music to His ears . . . because I know he hears all our prayers . . . even while He is resting! Do angels rest?

I seem to have many questions.

Lord, I know that if I pick up the cross . . . the crown and the nails go with it. Please help me to carry the cross as far as You want me to go. I know that you will be with me every step of the way because You were the first to walk the path of life. Amen.

UNDERSTANDING

Rejection batters my heart and fear makes me retreat into a place of safety.

But where **is** safety?

Where do I retreat?

If I retreat into myself, I find that I am not much kinder than the people I retreat from. Laughter has its place, but laughter can be used as a tool of disgrace. To laugh in the face of a person in pain is to laugh as if you were someone who has no regard of another person's feelings.

Why did you laugh at a time when I shared a painful part of my life?

I did not laugh with you . . . I retreated into myself where the laughter of the past resonated through my empty halls of memories. As I walked through those empty halls, a door opened and the warmth of forgiveness flooded the cold walls surrounding me. A friend extended his hand and I saw understanding within his face. I hesitated for a moment and then I took the hand of Forgiveness.

Thank you Lord for the warmth of your Forgiveness. Without your Forgiveness I certainly would be lost within the halls of my cold memories. Amen.

1 John 4:10-12 NRSV

In this is love, not that we loved God but that he loved us and sent his Son to be the atoning sacrifice for our sins. Beloved, since God loved us so much, we also ought to love one another. No one has ever seen God; if we love one another, God lives in us, and his love is perfected in us.

Father in Heaven,
Forgive me for making so many messes. I have such a talent for doing these things. Thank you for going behind me and binding the broken pieces together again. I know you can use all things for good. Thank you Lord. Amen.

Lord. I will walk into the night. I will follow the star that You have placed before me. What joy I will find at the end of my journey! Amen.

PASTORS

The Pastor of my church spoke loud and clear with a message that was uplifting and inspiring to me. Later, as I sat quietly reflecting on his message, I realized that we sometimes forget our Pastors are people just like ourselves. We often look at them in a different way than we look at our neighbors and friends.

They are our neighbors! They are our friends!

And yet, we seem to expect so much from them. We seem to forget that they have needs just like we do. They get sick just like we do. They have good days as well as days which are not so good. Most of them have families just like our families, which require their attention and yet, they always seem to be able to fit us into their busy schedule.

Let us remember the Pastors of our churches and their families today.

Reach out to them!

Let them know we love them as a friend and neighbor as well as the Pastors of our churches.

Ephesians 4:11 NAS
And He gave some as apostles, and some as prophets, and some as evangelists, and some as pastors and teachers.

YOU ARE

Are you still there Lord?
Yes, I can see that you are.
I see the twinkle in your eye when I look at
The stars in the dark night sky.

Are you still there Lord?
Yes, I can see that you are.
I see your bright smile and hear you hum a tune
When I look at the sun.

Are you still there Lord? Yes, I can see that you are.
I see your quietness in a flower, a bee,
A prayer and a cross.

Are you still there Lord?
Yes, I can see that you are.
I see your excitement when I look at a child
Flying a kite on a blustery day.

Are you still there Lord?
Yes, I know that you are.
I can see that you are with me because I know that
You Are.

Psalm 108:4 NAS
  For Thy lovingkindness is great above the
heavens; And Thy truth reaches to the skies.

PAST EXPERIENCES

I must admit that it is **so** easy for me to get caught up in past experiences.

I really delight in letting people know that I am a clown.

Being a clown makes me feel a little special.

The only thing is that I am not clowning right now. I have only clowned once in three years! Does that mean that I am no longer a clown? I guess I am still a clown, but the season of clowning is, at the moment, memories of days gone by.

I guess I should ask **myself** a question that I find dancing within my thoughts. Let me share that question with you. I feel the Lord is asking me: "What are you doing now? Memories of the past are treasures of the heart, but what are you doing now? Look upon your treasures and choose the one shining brightly before you."

Memories of past experiences can be wonderful, but let us look at the gifts given to us by God and see which gift is shining brightly at this moment

Current memories quickly become past memories. Let us experience each day as it is.

1 Timothy 6:6 NLT
A Godlike life gives us much when we are happy for what we have.

DO NOT MISS THE GLORY

Psalm 131:1-3 NRSV
>*O LORD, my heart is not lifted up,*
>>*My eyes are not raised too high;*
>*I do not occupy myself with things*
>>*Too great and too marvelous for me.*
>*But I have calmed and quieted my soul,*
>>*Like a weaned child with its mother;*
>>*My soul is like the weaned child that is with*
>>*Me.*
>*O Israel, hope in the LORD*
>>*From this time on and forevermore.*

"Why is your heart not lifted up? Why are your eyes not lifted high into the heavens? Nothing is too marvelous for you. I have come that you may have life and have it abundantly." Saith the LORD GOD of heaven and earth.

Calm your soul. Quiet your soul. But do not cast your eyes unto the depth below the heavens for if you do . . . you will miss the glory of this day.

LEAVES

Two brown shriveled leaves clung to an otherwise bare limb.

Winter was nearly a thing of the past, but the brown leaves were unwilling to let go of the grip they had upon the branch. Then one spring morning the tree began to bring forth a new set of leaves. The new leaves were green and fresh. Flowers began to blossom and the two brown leaves were urged to release their grip of the past and allow the newness of life to come forth. You do the same.

> *Isaiah 55:12 NLT*
> *"You will go out with joy, and be led out in peace. The mountains and the hills will break out into sounds of joy before you. And all the trees of the field will clap their hands."*

JEREMIAH

The book of Jeremiah . . . within the pages of the Bible . . . is not an easy book to read. Some people do not like to read this book because of all the gloom within it.

Maybe we see more than what we **want** to see . . . Maybe we see a small part of ourselves. Yes, there **is** gloom within Jeremiah, but I have been studying Jeremiah and I have found some beautiful reflections of Light.

Let me share a few glimmers with you . . . for in the darkest of times . . . Jesus is with you and His Light shall be brought forth for all to see.

In Jeremiah 1:5 God reminds Jeremiah that he was known to God before Jeremiah was even born. The Bible says: *"Before I formed you in the womb I knew you, and before you were born I consecrated you; and I appointed you a prophet to the nations."* If God knew Jeremiah that closely, why do we think He would not do the same for each of us? So it is with everyone.

Jeremiah 8:5 reminds us that backsliding is nothing new. We all tend to backslide somewhat at times. When we find ourselves backsliding, return to the Word of God, ask God for forgiveness and know that we are forgiven.

Jeremiah 29:11 is one of my favorite passages from Jeremiah. I am sure that we have all held fast to this scripture at some point in our lives. *"For I know the plans I have for you, says the LORD, plans for welfare and not for evil, to give you a future and a hope."* How comforting it is to me to know that God cares enough about me to give me a future with hope. I will turn from evil unless I am to stand against evil with the sword given to me.

I challenge you to read the book of Jeremiah. What bits of Light might you find within the folds of each chapter?

Jeremiah 8:5 RSV
  "Why then has this people turned away in perpetual backsliding? They hold fast to deceit, they refuse to return."

QUIET THOUGHT

I was in quiet thought.

I began thinking about things that meant a lot to me.

As I thought about these things, I saw a sunrise before me. The sunrise was beautiful because I was at the beach. The waves from the ocean were gentle and the water was warm. I wanted to remain and feel the breeze that blew my hair into interesting shapes. A friend came to me from somewhere within the sunrise. He greeted me with a warm smile. I asked him about what I saw before me. He said "What one sees as worthwhile another casts it into the sea of life never giving it another thought until the sea brings it back to them upon the waves of a sunrise. What do you view as worthwhile?"

Lord, thank you for sunrises and all the different things we see as worthwhile. Amen.

1 Peter 3:4 RSV
...but let it be the hidden person of the heart with the imperishable jewel of a gentle and quiet spirit, which in God's sight is very precious.

EXPLORE BOTH

I saw the universe before me.

The stars and planet were beyond all of my thinking. As I watched the beauty before me, I saw a heart appear within its beauty and I wondered about what was placed before me. A friend saw my wonderment and said, "Beyond the love of one's own heart is found the Love of the Universe. Within the love of one's heart is found the Love of the Universe. Explore both." Amen.

Lord, help me to explore all you have placed before me. Amen.

Ephesians 4:10 NIV
He who descended is the very one who ascended higher than all the heavens, in order to fill the whole universe.

A BASKET OF MEMORIES

I have a basket of memories.

My son thinks it is just a basket of old stuffed toys. To me it is a basket of memories.

In the basket are two small rabbits. The rabbits were given to my boys at Easter when the boys were small enough to enjoy a stuffed toy. Those rabbits are worn and shabby, but they make me smile.

One toy in the basket, I created from an old dress. I made toys for children that might need something to hug, but it was my son that wanted to hug this handmade creation and so, that toy rests in my basket.

I pick up my grandsons first teddy bear. As I look into his eyes, I remember how I retrieved him from a yard sale family members were having. To others he was a toy my grandson had outgrown. To me the little bear was timeless.

Another bear lives in my basket. He has no ears. My dog, Maggie, mistook the little bear as a toy she could play with. My son asks why I do not throw the bear into the trash. I reply "Nobody would love him in his condition and the trash seems so final to me."

There are two more stuffed animals in my basket of memories. They have no background of memories for me other than I rescued them from a pile of other unwanted toys at a church Bazaar. The toys at the Bazaar were unwanted by others. They were piled, one upon the other, in a heap of sorrow and sadness . . . waiting to be loved. Jesus rescued me from a pile of sorrow and pain. Jesus saved me from a future of hopelessness and He gave me a modest, but secure home.

Today, the toys rest in their home which is modest, but secure. They will stay in my basket of memories until I no longer am able to hold them in my arms . . . then, I pray someone will rescue them from a pile of unwanted items . . . just as I was saved from my sorrows.

Thank you Lord Jesus for saving me from myself. Amen.

Acts 15:11-12 NRSV

"On the contrary, we believe that we will be saved through the grace of the Lord Jesus, just as they will."

The whole assembly kept silence, and listened to Barnabas and Paul as they told of all the signs and wonders that God had done through them among the Gentiles.

THE NAME OF JESUS

Proverbs 18:10 NIV
The name of the LORD is a strong tower; the
righteous run to it and are safe.

I feel a sense of comfort when I read the scripture above.

All I have to do is say the name of Jesus and know that I am safe . . . For the **name** of Jesus is strong and powerful. When trouble, sorrow, sadness, fear and any other "things of the world" seem to overwhelm you, simply say His name. Strength and power and all understandings are within the name of Jesus. No other name can stand before Jesus and survive, but the righteous is sheltered within the name they utter in the name of the Lord. Amen.

FORGIVEN

The Lord has placed within me all that He wants me to be.

If I am able to achieve but a fraction of it, I have been able to touch His hand. And when I look into His eyes, I know that He has forgiven me for that which I have not fulfilled.

Thank you my Lord for all you have placed within me. Thank you my Lord for forgiving me for all I have not done. Amen.

Within my thoughts I heard: "I have forgiven you once . . . that is enough. So it is with all My children."

1 John 2:12 NKJV
I write to you, little children, Because your sins are forgiven you for His name's sake.

"DOING SOMETHING"

Isaiah 35:1-2 NIV

> *The desert and the parched land will be glad; the wilderness will rejoice and blossom. Like the crocus, it will burst into bloom; it will rejoice greatly and shout for joy. The glory of Lebanon will be given to it, the splendor of Carmel and Sharon; they will see the glory of the LORD, the splendor of our God.*

So often we feel that we must be constantly "doing something" in order to be doing the Lord's work. Not true!

Why do we think this way?

When we are constantly "doing something," we fail to see the importance of God's presence in our resting times. If you are a person like me, you may not know what a resting time might look like. Let me explain what a resting time might look like: Resting times are those times when we are not over committed with meetings, work and people. Resting times are times when we quietly talk to the Lord.

When do you take time to talk to the Lord? Not wanting something. Not running before Him. Not Expecting Him to do and do and do . . . whatever you want Him to do, but just talking to Him.

The Lord went into the mountains and deserts for his quiet times and we need to remember that He is walking in those same places today. Although the Lord is found in the wilderness places of life, He is also found where you are willing to meet Him. He is waiting to help us during our times in the deserts . . . in the wilderness . . . no matter where the wilderness may be.

We need to view these times as quiet times and rest in the Lord for He is with us always. He will bring us into our promised land when the time is right and just as He provided for our ancestors . . . He will provide for us.

Thank you Lord. Amen.

TRULY FREE?

I have heard people say that the best things in life are free.

In many ways, that statement is a true statement, but free can come with a cost. Does this statement sound like a contradiction to you? If you said yes, I agree. In many ways it is a contradiction, but in many ways it is not. Allow me to give you an example.

This is an example I found within my thinking:

"Looking upon the glorious beauty of a garden is free, but the cost of the garden is seen by the Creator that created it."

Did I hear you say that wild flowers are free to those passing them upon the roads of life?

Well, are wild flowers truly free?

Remember . . . even wild flowers need sun, water and nourished soil.

The only thing that is **truly free** is God's grace. As you extend grace to others . . . you receive more grace from God.

> Acts 16:26 NIV
> Suddenly there was such a violent earthquake that the foundations of the prison were shaken. At once all the prison doors flew open, and everybody's chains came loose.

WINGS

I sometimes grumble about my hair. I have enough curl in my hair that when the weather is humid, the hair over my ears flip upward. Then again, many times, there does not seem to be any rhyme or reason why my curls appear! I refer to those curls as "my wings."

My wings can be a challenge for me when they seem unruly and do not want to submit to my controlling them. Do you suppose God feels the same way about us when we want to do things our way instead of His way?

As I tried to control my wings, I could feel God smiling upon me as He said: "Wings are good at times. They help you to fly."

Thank you Lord for wings. Amen.

Psalm 55:6 KJV
> *And I said, Oh that I had wings like a dove!*
> *For then would I fly away, and be at rest.*

HOW TRUE

I saw a friend before me. I recognized her and smiled. She is a friend I can talk to, laugh with and share my life with. I smile each time I think of her. It is so good to have a friend like this. I thank God for bringing this friend into my life.

As I saw my friend walk away, I felt another friend beside me. He smiled. We watched as my friend walked into the distance. Silence was beautiful. Words were not needed, but they were welcomed when he said: "The depth of a friendship is not often known, but felt."

How true his words are to me.

As I reflected upon all I saw and felt, I realized how much I treasure the friendship of the friend I saw before me.

Then I wondered about the rest of my life. I had to ask myself: "How often do I look upon the image of Jesus with the same feelings as I look at my precious friend? How often do I feel the depth of His friendship?"

I must admit . . . Not often enough!

Forgive me my Lord Jesus.
Forgive me for I know I am precious in Your sight. Amen.

Proverbs 18:24 RSV
> *There are friends who pretend to be friends, but there is a friend who sticks closer than a brother.*

CROWDS REJOICE!

Dance my friends.
Dance with joy.
The Bridegroom's come
To man from boy.

When dancing's done
You're not alone.
God is there
To see you home.

So crowds rejoice.
The times arrived.
God's gift of love
Is by your side.

Matthew 25:6 RSV
But at midnight there was a cry. 'Behold, the bridegroom! Come out to meet him'.

GO TO THE GARDEN

Go to the garden to pray.

Listen to the voice of God.

Feel His breath and know the power of creation.

Isaiah 28:6 NLT
    For his God tells him what to do and teaches him the right way.